Made in United States
North Haven, CT
26 September 2024

57975551R00057